River Writing

PRINCETON SERIES OF CONTEMPORARY POETS

For other books in the series, see page 61.

River Writing

An Eno Journal

JAMES APPLEWHITE

PRINCETON UNIVERSITY PRESS

Published by Princeton University Press, 41 William Street,
Princeton, New Jersey 08540
In the United Kingdom: Princeton University Press,
Guildford, Surrey

Library of Congress Cataloging in Publication Data will be
found on the last printed page of this book

ISBN 0-691-06726-0 (cloth)   0-691-01442-6 (pbk.)

Publication of this book has been aided by the Lacy Lockert
Fund of Princeton University Press

This book has been composed in Linotron Aldus

Clothbound editions of Princeton University Press books
are printed on acid-free paper, and binding materials are
chosen for strength and durability. Paperbacks,
although satisfactory for personal collections, are not
usually suitable for library rebinding.

Printed in the United States of America by Princeton
University Press, Princeton, New Jersey

for Margaret Nygard
and the Association for the Preservation
of the Eno River

ACKNOWLEDGMENTS

Some of these poems were first published in the following magazines, to whose editors grateful acknowledgment is made: *Southern Poetry Review; Nomad; Kenyon Review; The Southern Review; Blue Unicorn; New Virginia Review; The Weymouth Reader; Carolina Quarterly; The Archive.*

CONTENTS

World's Shoulder, Turning   3

The Ford   4

Crossing on Cables   5

Constructing the River   6

Just Rain   7

Tree of Babel   8

A Wash of Words   10

Clear Winter   11

River Within/Without   13

Winds of These Times   14

Like a Body in the River   15

The Sense of Light   16

When the Night Falls   17

Miles to Go   18

The Snow's Code   19

The Text of the Sun   21

River Sequence   23

In Sight of the Self   24

The Hard Role   26

Glassed by the Cold   28

Buzzard's Roost   29

An Orphaned Voice   31

Late February   32

House of Seasons   33

The Sun's Tone   34

The Other, Nature 35

The Water-Machine 36

The Sex of Divinity 37

Light Beyond Thought 38

Out of My Circle 39

Prayer for My Son 41

The Corridor 42

Observing the Sun 44

The Bison 46

Bridge Back Toward the South 49

Driving Toward Cairo 50

Rivers 51

The Self, that Dark Star 52

Riding the Thunder 53

Thin Air on a Winter Day 54

The Consciousness-Glass 56

The Powerline Cut 57

Sleeping with Stars and Bulbs, Time
    and Its Signs 58

River Writing

But is not the desire for a center, as a function of play itself, the indestructible itself? And in the repetition or return of play, how could the phantom of the center not call to us?—JACQUES DERRIDA

Literary history has generally labeled "primitivist," "naturalistic," or even pantheistic the first modern writers to have put into question, in the language of poetry, the ontological priority of the sensory object. We are only beginning to understand how this oscillation in the status of the image is linked to the crisis that leaves the poetry of today under a steady threat of extinction.
—PAUL DE MAN

World's Shoulder, Turning

A rock of the bulk of a house leaned out
From bank across the creek—as if earth were still
In the making. Through the weed screen, I noticed
How light had lessened, mountain laurel beyond
Submerged in slope-shadow. Going back, I felt white
Quartz and the bone of a bracket mushroom
Shine their beams at me. The bouquet of huckleberry
Leaves I picked seemed tiny tropical fish.
They floated on their stems as I ran, and I
Added bleached grasses like sea oats, a few
Fronds of fern. I ran lightened in the gloom
By the scarlet and tan like a torch in my hand.
Yesterday I'd seen the sun, a scoured
Copper pan, shine through pines, from a bend
Of the high shouldering trail where the horizon
Falls away. I remembered the light's raying,
Like magnetized metallic dust. I felt all
These bright things—huckleberry stems and sea oats,
Quartz rocks and mushroom—held in the field
Of sun now down below shoulder of the world's turning.

The Ford

Today the air was mist, the river full
Bank to bank with fog. The time
Grows near the birth of Christ.
Because of the solstice. Because
We see a new year like a spark
In these short, dark days. Today
I felt released by the past. I passed
The hill where ruts made by wagons
To the mill seemed Civil War breastworks.
The past was only rock from
A wall, a chimney fallen in the woodland
Of *now*. In the rain, everything
Shone green.

Crossing on Cables

I'd passed the cable crossing, thinking it too late,
Until stopped by a movement in bushes. Squirrels?
A deer? I couldn't hear more. The two-story
Boulder near the river bulked gray under
Mountain laurel. I climbed the tree that held the cables
And slid my feet over water, steadied by the strand above.

The landing led up through a staircase crevice
To a ledge giving vantage over a rippled bend.
The rock-grain felt rough as tree bark, the top
Pitted and peaked like a topographical map
Of the continent. The hundreds-of-thousands-of-years-old
Shelf shone gray-green with lichen, mossed
In spots like forests seen from space. Resting,
My hand supporting me, I felt a cold slow
Pulse pushing between my bone and the granite.

Constructing the River

The sequences of the river write themselves
Anew every day. It is a flow which dries
In lines from my pen. Fine dogwood twigs
End in periods of buds, limb-type prints
Phonemes of foam on air. Words are things.
I feel them in my brain's blood, forming with my
Running. I am accompanied through a narrowing
Where path comes close to rocky shallows by a
Continuous murmuring of the many streams' tongues
The rapids form. I use *foam, stream,* and *tongue*
For their sound. So language refers to itself.
Millipede with tail in its mouth, it circles
In these woods and every word is a leg touching
Water or tree. The cliff shows an intrusion of quartz,
Crystalline vein continuing even where
Softer stone has rotted to loam. Word is not
Object but both exist and align. This poem
I am writing is not precisely the one in my head
As I was running. This presence is an illusion.
The relation between word-thing and quartz vein
Is something seen, clear air, quintessential
As metaphor. It was not there before. Poor
As we are, this affluent gleam at the speed
Of light vibrates between noun and thing, almost
Joining them. Grandsons of Freud, we handle
The mental toy, make it disappear like mother,
Fort/da, fort/da. We visit our own funerals with
Huck Finn. The word-river cherishes time that was,
That is, that will never again be. Is elegy.

Just Rain

The steady rain grew colder as I ran.
Honeysuckle crowding across the path sopped
My shoe tops with water. The river was
Louder than ever, a continuous crescendo,
A racing flow into frothing combers.
The current's galloping took over, thought
Forced to concentrate on the path's ledge
That offered an easy slide. To go under
The tan moil and hurry with small logs
Riding it bareback seemed, to my absent
Mind, attractive. Like call of the distance
Below a precipice. Cold and uncomfortable
Rain doesn't make one's possession of self
More intense. Mind wanders to memories
Of summer, close warm smells fill the
Breath. Raw is the word for the river. I
Regretted disturbing the small birds pecking
By the ford. I lay down in weeds at
The abandoned homestead, to feel what it's
Like being dead. Rain felt pure on my face.

Tree of Babel

A green air freshened from cedar
And holly. The river's metal
Reflection shone molten.
Rocks, washed of silt,
Left the mind rinsed.
The cloth in a fork,
Like a scrap tacked to fact
From dream, was gone.
From the shore I'd crossed to by cable,
I looked back at people
Hiking on Sunday.
I waved before fading
Into trees. The boot print
I found in a clearing
(Like Friday coming on Crusoe)
Stunned me. A hundred yards on,
An ancient, forked beech
Carved with illegible
Letters seemed text
To the living story
Of abandoned rows under trees.
A scribble of vines loaded
My head like a dictionary's
Waste heap.
Beyond the written beech,
An ice-white sycamore
Spired air
With absolute moment.
I discovered the illusion

Newly. The pool of perception
Inked only by branches
Seemed garden before
Transgression, flood high over
The Babel tower. I came
Home from this year
Made new with only a happy
Headache, a thorn in my finger.

A Wash of Words

Leaden, I surprised the sun,
A great copper pan
Through crowns of pines.
It weighed its ton
On the path, that inclined
Toward it with my breath.
I could run. I tasted
Glistening over my tongue
The sound-feel *young*:
Not a property of me
Or of the river, but of
Its flash upon the mirror
That beholds it.
All the way to the bridge,
I ran through airs
And humidities like sheets
Hung on a line. Breathed
Washed accents of language.

Clear Winter

Confusion of seasons is over.
Today was clear winter.
Light that on trunks seemed warm
Looked bleak and bare
On chill limbs high in chill air.
I saw bodies of trees
Piled mercilessly by past
High water, crotch-chunk
Of one upon trunk of another.
Angular cedars, their crowns
Thinned of needles by drought,
Seemed a desert tribe
Overtaken by an angel of death.
Finally I climbed clear
Of the valley which memory
Stocked with its proxy
Corpses. I saw air
In its isolation now pure.
We are unable to endure
This light the cold whets to steel.
I stood above river land
And hypothesized the being
We cannot understand, who
Begins things with flame of a star.
Who is the zero far dark.
I sniffed for scent of some smoke,
For coffee, leaf-smolder or

Cigarette odor. All unendurably
Absent. I turned toward home,
Alone as a pane of ice
The keen sun shines through.
I kissed my warm wife
And under the first star
Gathered cedar for a fire.

River Within/Without

Today, a rime of ice on the path.
I make metaphor of water.
Or simply record
The figures of the river.
The one who runs and is
Aware is wrapped in the same
Light and air as the trees.
A bend curves closer to words.
Mind lamps back a damp
Flash of language. Verbs,
Rubbed on rocks, take a fresh
Edge. The interlinked spillage
Of phonemes, sliding, signifying
Are made to name by things
Like underwater dams. Rock ledge
Roils a print, the ripple-shine of
Current like vowel/consonant.
I palm the oak's bark.
Noun *tree*. Governs verb *to be*.
Two rivers are flowing this poem.

Winds of These Times

Today with ice by the path, I let
The wind bare my pain. Most of the run
Was numb. Nothing would come until
I'd climbed up the slope from Pea Creek.
From the powerline cut, the image
I may have been seeking: two trees
Crushed into an embrace. In the winds
Of these times, I hardly know who
Is uprooted. The thick-legged woman
With her Labrador on the other side
Of the river pleased me. Cold makes
Friends of a stranger. Why not of a lover?
Toppled together, we break each other.

Like a Body in the River

The atmosphere was bitter mist—my nerves
Worse than the weather. I buttoned on
A Bean guide jacket, laced rubber foot
Boots. Running on the slushy bank felt
Childishly barefoot. I ran without thought.
A heavy plop, and circles in the river marked
A beaver I'd surprised. I stopped to watch
Its seal-like head in the sledding current,
Its outraged eye. The cocoa water grew
Darker, with bass thumps and drowning
Percussions. The river bobbled with nightmare.
Turgid screams drove at me out of my dreaming
Remembrance—tight as wire lines the bats
Stitched in the net of branches. I'd seen,
On a figure at a stoplight, the face
Of my friend's dead wife. Felt lost.
The sepia light rusted toward oblivion
As I groped toward home in grief.

The Sense of Light

I run in an unmoving pane
That accompanies my face, a beam
Like a stream standing still—
While vines and tree trunks flow
Furiously. Though bronze through the lens
Of sun in afternoons, this other sun
Has no tone. The father I saw,
Hovering over his toddler, will
Hold the umbrella and pull down shades
In vain. This absolute light X-rays
Walls, transparent cliff that
Crowds us to the edge of space.
Overexposure thins the scenes
Of our lives. It is a summer sun
In which we dream by the river,
Scheming for constancy, changing.

When the Night Falls

I crossed on the cables when it was late
To look at what I thought was a boat.
Earlier I'd seen the air illuminate
A white sycamore, thought even more
Marvelous the scene in my brain—
That the two were one. But not
For long. Still, given the path's aim,
The young will see it almost the same.
The painting will be similar, with different
Signature in the corner. Whenever I
Imagine being dead, I can't see
The world without an angle. My foot
Finds air instead of path, I stumble and
Lose my breath. I feel the phenomenology
Of self, no name of Applewhite, only bushes
And briars and undetermined shapes in the night—
Feel dissociate, and *far*. I'm almost out
Of the picture. The picture remains. Howl
From dog or owl comes scrambled and haunting.
The seat from a junked truck, one end
Sunk in ice near the bank, proves the boat
I'd thought. I find I've caught my leg
On the old barbed wire below the cable.
I hurry across hand over hand, almost
Take a tumble in the ice-crusted river.
The sycamore lighted by consciousness returns.
I'll run the sun while there is time.

Miles to Go

Seeing and hearing expanded today.
I came into a beech grove open
Like a clearing. The ferns in folds
Of Pea Creek's valley walls shone
Clean through breath-misting overcast.
The slope made a large room.
Leaves were a rug of loam.
Holly punctuated its holiday welcome
With red dots coding bent green.
Rocks under the grape-pulp current
Seemed forms half-seen
Through sleep. The words like
A taste on the tongue: *brown, lie down.*

The Snow's Code

A cedar like a lancet window
Down the snow-loaded aisles seemed
A Black Forest icon. Hoffmann or Hans
Christian Andersen. Trees feathered
Softly swan-white on gray duck bark.
Cold was cruel, seventeen degrees
When I set out. I kept dreaming
Through branches the Christmas scene
On campus. Spires and roofs of Trinity
Lifted their outline. Gold electric
Lights from the great hall, sharpened
By arches, cut into the night—
Glowed a cold where our frost-breaths
Praised Christ. These structures of stone
And word are our imperial
Burdens, skylines of Oxford-ideal
Built past our ability to fulfill
Them, fractious and self-interested
As we are, though moved by Handel,
The refectory's leaded panes, a star.
Yet Jane Goodall's chimp that killed
Its brother ape proves Cain
Again in a different text. We would
Be murderous still, only poorer,
Without our words, our stones of grandeur.
Retracing tracks toward home, I

See holly and cedar dotted and
Dashed with snow, the pagan coding
Behind our Christian crèche. A child,
I feel the North cut nearer, zero wind
Sing me the tale of the Erlking.

The Text of the Sun

Birds stir in basketry bushes
As I brush by. Each kind its own
Tongue. Wrens whet bills on wind.
Quail recall their double notes
From summer, questioning themselves.
The psyche finds almost enough, here
With rapids, the birds' near-language.
I have no eyes I am aware of,
Only sights in sequence of *root*, then *log*.
And wind that cools itself
On the outside of breath. This iced
Sheer loneliness feels *known*.
I look too suddenly sunward.
A flame-bubble floats
On the flow of my motion.
It prints its gold dot
In sight. Molten balloon,
Platinum sun-sign
(Father, erasure, mirror), you
Center this text of light.

Afterimage, a tarnished coin,
Projects onto clay and pine straw.
A zero circles the tight
Cell of self. I see
Consciousness in what is not.
In continuous nature, I am
One. Blind son.
The sunset, leveling

Across the river, catches
Only top branches.
The wavering envelope of gasses
Distorts, descends: hole
From which identity issues.

River Sequence

Two kingfishers flew as a blue
Ice smear over water. Mother
Grows farther and farther from
Me in nature. Nature stands nearer.
Yet this world opposes our will and
Our identity. Her bronchial spasms
Alarm, the heart goes irregularly.
Where will I find her later? The body
Is base of each metaphor, vehicle
Upon which the spirit mounts
Its tenor. Our objective presence
Is skin and breath and gesture,
Flesh our reference-text and key
For the signs' codes exposing
Character. Will I find, in sky
Lined by limbs, the type to spell her?
Where else shall I look for
The gray Athena-eyes she turned
Upon her satisfied questioner,
Child who desired again every
Story the days had provided?
Do I see tall building in the trees?
It is only the pines' homes. Then
Stone of the nineteenth-century mill,
Broken gate where the stream
Went, when it had turned the wheel,
Free in its own will.

In Sight of the Self

Current from rain last night
Crushes past, rapids with separate
Cordings like glistening muscle.
A lecture has made me late
But I feel at home in my house
Of clothes, poncho an envelope
Sealing heat. The dim chasm
Between banks of trees flows
With fog in the rain. I run
An inchoate terrain as in
Dreams, the soaked path slick
As shit, air half water, my
Breath only puff of fog and the
River a pavement of light
The mist diffuses. I ask
Myself what I am doing
Here in the night, if anyone
I know would recognize
The person they give my name.
I have left my poncho on
A limb and run on, too warm.
Now I return and find it
Like something hung by current,
Apart from me, yet shape of
A body. As the rain comes
Harder, I resume that part
Of myself, that house of breath.
Light grows late, shape of
The path approximate. I remember

A circular erasure
From seeing the sun. The rain
Spreads around its sound
In rings, as from the pebble
In a pond. I am the center
That drops out of sight:
Bullseye everything aims at,
Dot of the target.

The Hard Role

Yesterday's river was too raw
For writing. Banks had been swept
By a night current ready to drown
Any walker. Logs were pitched on rocks,
Rain's will still ran in a giant
Thrust of tawny flooding, waves
Cresting continually behind islands
Of stone. Was it the tight reins
Of those horse drivers, our frontier
Fathers, the Bear Bryants and John Waynes,
That have drawn us toward muddy water?
Or is this the view of the loser
In the family romance? I wondered
Saturday at the slab fingers of my father,
Blunted of a joint by an air compressor,
As they soothed mother's brow to the sigh
Of her respirator. Maybe our native
Will is to run wild with the current,
As yesterday I saw the young man's
Child charging downhill toward
The ford. Father, I remember, you
Caught me back from my run
Toward water, that night of the carnival,
And I off the carrousel, drunk
With turning, running over the sand.
Perhaps we have to have our role
Capture us from behind, hard hand
Counter to feeling. Poor soul, poor
Hole in sight, who puts on pants

Or dress with flesh, to recognize
No self in any guise. I run
Into the current of sensation,
A thrust without face or place
Except in flux and flash
Of the river.

Glassed by the Cold

Bushes bow in the path, specimens
In this temporary museum, each in
Its ice case. Any tree needled or leaved
Is bent as under a weight of light.
The news will label this *ice storm*
But here by the Eno it does no harm—
Some break but most will endure this
Intricate aureole like each kind's form
Made clearer than it can bear. With
Mist in the air and a temperature just
Below freezing, I feel almost dry.
Still, the path is too slickly liquid
To keep my Bean boots' chained prints. Yet
These trees are glassed by an art that is
Diamond-cut in the pane of my breath—
Cased by a shine made hard, a moment.
Beeches toward the ford are scribed
As by an engraver in silver: cold,
To keep blood-impulse of the river.

Buzzard's Roost

As the ball world falls
Away downhill, only one point
Is flat: this moment.
Riding the quickly turning
Earth, I am spun into night.
Conception would run
In abstract strides,
Measuring distance
Like a draftsman's compass.
But below this geometer's
Diagram, the river is plowed
Into a harvest of flashes.
Its hot brilliance
Into peripheral vision
Stains with afterimage.
The current is my personal
Distance, the crooked going
That colors the straight light
With error. Crossing the cable,
I narrow my footing to one line.
On the farther side, I climb
The two-story house of stone,
Stand alone in a height
Of pure illumination. I see the Eno
Wrinkling and sliding
Fifty feet below, wearing
Reflection like sweat
On skin. The moment
Like a statue passes,

I kneel, dizzy, see
Moss in an ice-rimmed cup
Of rock. I walk the cable back,
Continue my narrow strand
Of time, composing
Its form
Line by line.

An Orphaned Voice

I came down to the swollen river.
Kingfisher stretched his straight flight
Away, white-collared, uniform priest
Of waters. I was left to the rapids'
Idiot merriment, fat splash and
Unconscious laughter. *Full. Full. I am
Always young.* Left alone to give
The torrent tongue, I was swept
Along in sympathy, no head in sight
Above the current's bucking bed:
Quilt of cream foam and sediment.
Whatever circles made by turtle or
Beaver had melted. Forms
Plunged back underwater. In that wet
Rattle I listened hard for words
Of a father. Finally, from trees, came
The kingfisher's blue, electric chatter.

Late February

I run uphill to bright air,
Feeling the earth round underneath
My feet. Spun inconceivably
Rapidly from all I hold dear—
Letters and poems and love I
Should have made better—I say
What's done is done. And will be
Again tomorrow. Past limbs
I catch glimpse of the sun's
Heat-melt: elastic pupil
Flaring our lives into their
Papery being. From this cyclops I
Ask only energy of concentration—
For my one run toward its round.
Back on the ridge, I merge my
Face with the jonquils' chill,
Delighted yellow: petals spread,
Blown back as by the speed of light.

House of Seasons

Frost has browned these vines
That mound in the corner of vision, like
Forms from a dream. They don't determine
Decoration. October is buttoned by an
Aster's purple. Spring, so much closer,
Ignites in trout lilies' match flames,
Hepatica's blue porcelain. It is
In love, it is *being*. Jonquils
At the home site roofed only by evening
Greet me above the briared floor—
Sweet as, after long flight, the sight
Of my wife. By the river, I remember
How driving with my father
I'd imagine outside a giant figure
Stride-by-stride pacing the car. I run
Within that shadow, then return to the farm
Of only jonquils. A grown man, I bow
To the widows in yellow. As my nail
Snaps stems tense with sap,
I wonder who planted them—
Then walk with my wand of bloom
Home to the living woman I love.

The Sun's Tone

Today I did not catch the sun,
No flash from rapids imprinting
Image, fresh source of words. Instead,
Near the grave of Catharine Dunnagan—
Born Mch. 7 1826
Died Jan. 6 1914
On a stone in an overgrown clearing—
I collected jonquils, their yellower centers
Bells of color. The tense source I had
Missed vibrated through stems as I
Plucked them, a clear tone of bloom
Sounding in my hand as I ran.

The Other, Nature

A boy growing up beside the farms,
I felt as lonely as the mourning dove
Suggested: for something out of reach, in sleep,
Or in the next county. Today I have visited
The far river bank: like being in a different
Century. Here as I climb the trail toward
Home, a dog's bark, distant in this gloom,
Sounds hollow enough for time, as it siphons
My life down its drain. The ridge
Bulked ponderously above, granite folds
Altering perspectives. A beech slope
Surrounded one maple, the twigs a blond spray.
I had wandered like a returning spirit.
Trout lily carpeted the flats, below ruin
Of a dam, in that ghost town of business,
Where a mill wheel had turned. These flowers—
More beautiful than furniture or dishes,
Yet inconsequential, gone with a glance—
Made me sigh. When I returned to the maple's
Hill, I ascended into sight of the river,
To the side of the tree. Its trunk was double,
Rough-barked, vital, gesturing
Upward: each bud a spark. I circled
Its boles in my arms. I touched cheek
To the inanimate fork, in a gesture only I
Will always remember.

The Water-Machine

What moves is the river's bottom layer.
It carries an aura, an envelope of continuing
Air, here where the path has disappeared in
The seamless grasses, the honeysuckle tangle.
Webs break on my face, as I still follow
This elastic animal, infinitely divisible,
Whose plastic mass knifed by snags rejoins
And rejoins, a divided whole always going.
I catch the sun over my shoulder. A molten
Hole gauges my moments, levels through
Vectors of limbs. I look from the round
Run of space to the crooked path. The word
Uterus comes sinuously to my mouth. I
Feel my brain an organic machine that
Yearns. Cell-sacs light up in eddys.
This binary flicker of matter,
Like the live river, can drift
And breathe. Can mean.

The Sex of Divinity

The blooms have mostly gone
But rains have come. The river runs
Bright tan. June is almost
Upon us. I feel weak at first on
The trail in this third week after
My respiratory virus. The foliage has
Massed so as to make one imagine
Some fossil forest compacted to a coal
Of green. Leaves screen the sun
So I can endure its hard shine,
Its bead-bright splintering rattle.
The far bank yields a wild astilbe.
I see the sun whole, a transparent orb.
This androgyne is round as mind,
To illumine within and without.
I break spider webs as I run.
High on Buzzard's Roost, I look down
As on my shirt the hundreds
Of strands my chest has collected
Stretch and glisten, shirt of Nessus
Or Lilliput cables I break as
I breathe, giant in thought.
My small circumference has caught
Fire from the fierce eye shining
Its sexual round through leaves.

Light Beyond Thought

I wonder what summer I remember? I
Sit in shadow, where a dust of pollen
On waterfloor moves with the broom of wind.
And gnats gyrate, lighter than dust,
Fluff on the wrist of the river,
Jumping to its pulse. Spider webs float,
Dragonflies chase each other, and the sycamore
Leaning over from the opposite shore,
Its trunk in splotches like quarters,
Like camouflage, is almost silver. Its
Roots exposed by erosion flow
And mold like concrete, a scaffolding
Intricate as water in limestone—
Like the roots of memory. Mountain
Laurel blazes in flower. Green seems
To create its own meaning. This long
Day's sun, still high, seems frozen.
Glistens too richly to question.

Out of My Circle

Vines coil, dull in their greenness—
Three-leaved, poisonous. Turtles
In the ponds of bends
Slide under. A snake's shed
Skin and first blackberries
Mark beginning of summer.
Hepatica, foam flower,
No longer sign their names
With wands of bloom. The ego,
Not to grow ill, must
Go out of its circle. Dead
Water shrinks in the shape
Of a target, black-wet
Silt around it. Whatever
Life it surrounds now names
Itself with splash or wriggle.
In order not to grow ill,
I must travel. All biology
Stirs here in this womb of mud
But is not self-aware.
I must see my life from afar.
As I am driving westward,
Land through the windshield
Will hit a center it aims at:
Self that pivots horizons about
Its point. In sun on rocks
In the stream, I seem to feel
The wind of driving. Snake slips,

Half-seen, from the rock
Below my feet, pours his black
Length back into the river
Like a bitter drink. Not
To grow ill, we must learn to speak.

Prayer for My Son

The low river flows like smoked glass.
Small bass guard their nest. Next
To our house, the cardinals in their
Crabapple feed two open mouths.
Parents and offspring, we flex
And swing in this future's coming,
Mirror we look into only darkly.
My youngest is boarding an airplane
To a New York he's never seen.
Raised in such slumberous innocence
Of Bible schools and lemonade,
I adjust poorly to this thirst for
Fame, this electronic buzz prizing
Brilliance and murderers. Oh son,
Know that the psyche has its own
Fame, whether known or not, that
Soul can flame like feathers of a bird.
Grow into your own plumage, brightly,
So that any tree is a marvelous city.
I wave from here by this Indian Eno,
Whose lonely name I make known.

The Corridor

River's corridor winds the sun.
White hills in sky which thunder
Replenish its water. Dragonfly vanishes
And flashes, moving from shadow
To sun-shaft, hovering at reflections
On boulders. Like mirages from heat,
Like hallucinatory pieces of mirrors.
This is essential summer, a July
Sculptured by clouds' height and weight.
Pastures of grass with cattle, hills
Of trees, this gravel trail that connects
With roads the horses trod, lie
Prone under a lodestone sun. Its brightness
Drains us, as lines like iron filings
Rise toward rain. From a stone
In the middle of the stream, I see
This river's water as intensified clarity,
Watch a crayfish raise steel claws
Above this film he breathes, circling
As if dancing. Fingerling bass
Gather in the shallows, a family photograph,
Like my children in last week's surf-flash.
Who does not wish to be born
Of the one afternoon of full summer?
As the fierce light flares the weeds

With spontaneous being? While bass twitch
Quick in their plasma, aligned like
Needles with its current?
For a moment I see myself thus,
Of gold flesh and thought.

Yet these fingerlings remember no house
With corridor toward parents in shadow,
Their outline a tintype portrait. Lined with
Names in their Bible, I cannot belong
To this self-generated summer day.

Observing the Sun

Under clouds suspended over houses,
The sycamore's leaf-spray shadowed
My hand on a stone. Rails fenced corn
Against escape back to the farm. Cat birds
Teetered on the phone wire like children,
As doves perched too stolid and mournful higher
Even to make their cry. I felt
The loneliness of full summer,
Anyplace as close as anyplace else,
When routes on a map (called to mind
By roots) lost themselves into
Circuits underground. Passing cafés
And adobes, I will sense the life
Lines that sprout there at night, when palms
Dream, to tendril those foundations.
But driving by, I will never hear
The story of some Methodist minister's
Daughter, whose mother, a cripple,
Willed her the family at eighteen. I will
Never see the hurricane that drove her,
Later, from the three-room school
On the Pamlico River. Nor the orange
For the fisherman's son, like sun
On that horizon. But I will see windows,
See humans, read Indian lines
Around eyes, will feel the *where*
Of any place, the wheeling of our fathers
Under stars, on this hot-stone

Planetary merry-go-round
Filmed by the creation over lava.

I feel us as lightly aligned
As heads of the Queen Anne's lace,
Their congregation of angles.
Red sun, dilated, has us all
In its sights. Against its horizon,
I spread my arms like a road sign
To mark earth where we are.

The Bison

In the Tetons, hiking up Paintbrush Canyon,
I lifted up more than my weight with each
Step along that trail, with its long slopes
And switchbacks, its soil filled with round stones
From glaciers. Mount Woodring was immediately
Above to my right, through the lodgepole pines.
There above seven thousand feet, air tasted
Thin on the tongue. Vistas of Wyoming
Sagebrush, a dirt road that cut from the highway,
To run thirty miles toward the horizon,
Had drawn a topography more desolate than
My emptiness needed. A ground squirrel had narrowly
Escaped, where the pavement matted with bloody fur
Showed the jackrabbits' ignorance of shortest distances.
The map droned its miles of lines, the instinctive
Swerve I'd made, to miss a hawk taking off
Across the highway, waking me only a moment
From my doze among metamorphic strata,
Those fossil angles scattering the desert
In Silurian upthrusts, Triassic fractures—
Dinosaur names from childhood's picture book.
Beyond a cleft of shade, I saw a hawk arc
Suddenly from cliff's gloom, wing feathers
Translucent in that wall of illumination.
The great pane that held my walk shifted
Steadily nightward, like a mountain-tall
Transparent glacier whose yellow tone deepened.
In the canyon beyond the pines, Jenny Lake
Was aluminum in the moose grass of Jackson Hole.

Clouds seemed to scrape over the stone spires,
To attach for a moment, flags of breath-fog.
The monkshood was waist high, Indian paintbrush
Flaming in patches, and, higher, in wet ledges
By the cascade, villages of white colombine.
A backpacker returning said it was too late now
For Holly Lake. I went on faster, dry breath
Quick and the pulse beating lightly in my ears.
A French family passing through the cut
Above the falls said Holly Lake was not so far.
The teen-agers were long-legged, hairless, light
On the rocks as antelope. In the fern around
The next bend, the pink succulent flowers
Camped by the rapids turned all my breath
To bright color. I remembered the Continental Divide,
That bleak horizon beside the Interstate,
The Peterbilt diesels blasting up the one slope,
Coasting down the other. No higher trail in view.
No possibility of imagination's losing itself
Up some incline exceeding expectation.
But here the glaciers on the Teton walls
Let down their streamers of water, white
Feathers blowing in that late afternoon
Of all time. I inhaled that flame of wind,
Knew the Durham I would go back to,
The imperfect setting for my imperfect self,
Would be enough. Would be all that I could
Reach this afternoon, remembering the mist
At Colter Bay, above glacial Jackson Lake,

Whose water-ground stones of red and gray
And slate green were lined across their pitted
Smoothness with a layering beginning in
The Cretaceous sea. I made it as far as
Holly Lake, came down in the sunset and
Its afterglow to String Creek, where a mule deer,
Drinking, bounded away some paces, eyeing me
With black nose and tall ears focused,
Allowing me its world. In almost-night
On the road back toward the campground, the silhouette
Crossing the light had shoulders thicker than any moose.
The matted, godly brow, the eyes only implied
Below those headdress horns, configured an urge:
A shadow still alive with wildflowers, the craggy wind.

Bridge Back Toward the South

Saturday night, driving toward the Mississippi bridge
On Missouri highway fifty-one, drinking beer,
Listening to the country radio, four thousand
One hundred and forty-four miles
Newly on the odometer, I stop at a tavern
To ask my way across. The barmaid stretches
Her jeans with easy flesh and ignorance.
The one table of customers are all drunk.
A kid drinking Dr. Pepper alone at the bar
Explains how I should go. When I come
Into the diffused glow of lights from
The river not yet seen, that expands from
Below the road-level—like an air I could drive on—
I can almost forgive the South
For this ball of feeling in my throat.

Driving Toward Cairo

I've lost the route leading
Here. I know only this
Deep river, these barns and cornfields
And a telephone line—two wires
Between the spaced poles—to remind
Me of our connection and of our
Loneliness. And the church
Past the village of Anna, past
Jonesboro, where Lincoln debated,
Square small steeple transmitting
The sweet sad assurance of those
Hymns. The apple tree with
Green fruit, the crepe myrtle
Blazing, the double silos
As the sun comes out. This
Illinois landscape holds
A home I've never known.

Rivers

Campsites in Nebraska, Wyoming, Tennessee
Will never take the print of my shoulders
Again. Five-thousand-odd miles have
Wound into memory. I find it has rained.
Today, the gray silt in the Eno shows me
The body of the muddy Illinois.
When clouds pile reflections
On its face, it will imitate
The mighty Ohio. Clear, green,
It will be the Snake in Wyoming.
Oh Vermillion, Spoon, Meramec,
Tennessee, Caney Fork, Shoshone,
Missouri, Kanawha, Little Blue,
Cedar, Platte, Medicine Bow.
As the Eno runs in its same
Way, it catalogues your names.

The Self, that Dark Star

There in the Tetons at nine thousand feet,
The Eno thinned on my tongue.
Now that I am home, it is thinned
By autumn. As I walk the trail back,
Those time zones I've driven
Hover above my shoulders.
As I am spun to the East,
I taste their steel singing. No matter
How fast I run, a vacant land
Westward observes the last sun.
It may be that such land is my own:
Cheyenne, salted with hail, under
Bolts like the end.
The center of me empties, a cyclone's.
Like eyes which have stared at horizons.
I found desert and flood,
No ego-restoration. Perhaps
This hole in identity, this loss
Of self which is poetry,
This being like a collapsed sun hoarding
Its rays—is the *I* of me. If I am
A yearning, simply, a gravity—
If, star fathers who
Have erased me, I have no
Brighter surface—may these
Mountains and rivers, one bison, shine
Their denser radiation
As they vortex into your son.

Riding the Thunder

As I came out of the forest,
The film of dust from a truck
Scummed light. I saw a pond.
Gasoline stained a rainbow
Over water behind the engine.
Propeller shaft muscled way
Into a quiet yellow green. Then it
Started, then silence was never the same.
I rode on a red prow, held rope
The bull-boat clenched like a bit
In its teeth. It bucked, reared
Once, then planed. Water separated
By its prism rayed as in a spectrum:
Fresh as the names decreed by Adam.
Whips of drops hit my feet. An Evinrude
Bellowed its Logos, stirred
The grass plain to plowed vees.
Memories. I turned from the highway,
Ran the dirt trail through
Trees again, feet tripped
Where a bulldozer had printed its weight—
Had left its stink, like the bull that broached
Trace through a green unconscious
When a speedboat roared that Word.

Thin Air on a Winter Day

Settler or scholar, the idea first
Was of power: the words weighted like
Laws, the laws wrested from texts,
The cabins founded on clay, the logs
Peaked and notched, systems of corners extended.
The scriptures commanded, land listened
To the plough's lines, raised grudging corn,
Was quick to revert, cedar-wild after the mule.
All this cellar-hole, below these half-squared
Oak joists—poles with old bark—
Is past, is poetry, is force
Belonging to no one, emotion
Bequeathed by those who are gone.
A baby shoe, laceless, rests beside
The parent brogan. Antique brick
Holds a fingerprint, a shard of melted
Glass in the fireplace aches as if flame
Congealed. These present-day scholars in power,
These coercers of words, whose words
Are a creed, but not religion—let them
Huddle an afternoon on this ridge, this edge
Over river where the periwinkle and ivy
Grow greenest in shadow of headstones.
Let them wrestle with the jungle
Of this thought: that vines and briars
Hold nexuses of forces where human
Life has rooted. As I drive toward home,
A cedar at nightfall springs from two

Bleak chimneys, a nameless flame.
The birds that flutter reluctantly
Like tired heart muscle
Don't even whistle. Weather
Dismantles the cabins. Words
Carved in beech bark stretch and flake.
Earth is scorched by new wit. If it
Wants no intentions, let it marry time.
Two hundred years is a clarifying lens.

The Consciousness-Glass

The tree that disappeared,
Pinkly on the ridge as
I moved, flew a cloud
Like a flag in last
Sun—air in that *beyond*
Crystalline as a bell's
Tone. Breath close about
Felt soaked by the river.
Was frog-skin color, held
Sound of foam. Two zones
Met at the diaphragm.
Brass sun-grains draining
From the hourglass chest
Fell into a vanishing story
Murkier than this flowing.
A glass consciousness
Must be more solitary
Than a bubble on the water
Unless the narrative
Sponge of some unknowing
Layer is continuous
With all times. Can
Squeeze back, grain
By grain, the sun's
Bronze bonfire, horizonward,
Turning the cedars to iron.

The Powerline Cut

Walking the cut roots and persistent sumac,
I sensed the gray campus spires diminish
Behind, where a bulldozer huffed its muscle
Beside the hospital spreading like a cancer.
A ridge with plumed curves alive against
The glooming cedars stopped me—far from home,
Afoot, when light was scant. Poor clay
That the mechanical specters waded, abstract
As theorists, shelved this new South
Of semiconductor laboratories, universities
Run by corporations. The stems' givingness
Against the grudged soil set free, one and
By one, fluff seeds to fly as if mosquitoes.
I thought of those wagers of words, that any
Extension of knowledge is a reaching for power.
Broom sedge stood in the style of those
Who are moved by children, their hand-me-down
Clothes on the roadside, yielding to the tune
Of clay and moon. Its slant under evening,
Receptive to the wide air's elegy, sowed
Fields like amber grain but bearing nothing.

Sleeping with Stars and Bulbs, Time and Its Signs

Now the year is gone I lie proleptically
Down in the same winter in which I
Began to run. Trees taller than this pillow
Of earth their leaves feather is round
Stand above. Dreams falter near the fallen
Chimney stones, vines binding them to my
Forehead and to a cedar. In my tent that blocks
Orion, I listen with one ear against earth
For each jonquil bulb alive in the abandoned homestead.
The spading fork I hid in weeds two seasons ago
Is rusting quietly in the same time order as these
Relics of the astral family, whose rafters are outlined
By branches overhead. A brass hinge in subsoil swings
   their door
Upon a room full of space. China pieces cohere
Like stars in the Coalsack nebula. Each jonquil bulb
Sacked here begins to unsheathe its single green claw
Which will dig a yellow from night.
Flowers through my memory of their numbers
Gather the slope below us into one expanse,
Where the names of brothers cut in bark in 1911
Near the Model-T carcass unearth the artifacts
Of Henry Ford's century, recovering the pitted
Drive shaft from farm rows the trees have put
Back underfoot. I feel myself half-invisible, as thin
Against air as these brothers and their father and mother.
Taken back over by nature's left-handedness,

I turn over, heavily, in my bag. The arbitrary
Connectives of language, composted below me
With crockery and jawbone, stem in time
As between the bulb and its flower. All will come
Round again, will be sounded. Though the cleft hoof
Of each rock under my back symbolizes the final
Fact that will trip this body, self-damned
In time its dream, no doubt will pluck
My signs from signifying actually in their velvet
Bag below sleep. The bulbs I transplanted
To my own house will ring times in and out when
It also is a branch-sketched cinder of rafters.
Tonight, still, I expand in drowsiness,
To feel my huge shadow gravity-held,
On the physical basis of all poetry,
Nailed to earth's wheel by the stars.

PRINCETON SERIES OF CONTEMPORARY POETS

Returning Your Call, by Leonard Nathan
Sadness And Happiness, by Robert Pinsky
Burn Down the Icons, by Grace Schulman
Reservations, by James Richardson
The Double Witness, by Ben Belitt
Night Talk and Other Poems, by Richard Pevear
Listeners at the Breathing Place, by Gary Miranda
The Power to Change Geography, by Diana Ó Hehir
An Explanation of America, by Robert Pinsky
Signs and Wonders, by Carl Dennis
Walking Four Ways in the Wind, by John Allman
Hybrids of Plants and of Ghosts, by Jorie Graham
Movable Islands, by Debora Greger
Yellow Stars and Ice, by Susan Stewart
The Expectations of Light, by Pattiann Rogers
A Woman Under the Surface, by Alicia Ostriker
Visiting Rites, by Phyllis Janowitz
An Apology for Loving the Old Hymns, by Jordan Smith
Erosion, by Jorie Graham
Grace Period, by Gary Miranda
In the Absence of Horses, by Vicki Hearne
Whinny Moor Crossing, by Judith Moffett
The Late Wisconsin Spring, by John Koethe
A Drink at the Mirage, by Michael J. Rosen
Blessing, by Christopher Jane Corkery
The New World, by Frederick Turner
And, by Debora Greger
The Tradition, by A. F. Moritz
An Alternative to Speech, by David Lehman
Before Recollection, by Ann Lauterbach
Armenian Papers: Poems 1954-1984, by Harry Mathews
Selected Poems of Jay Wright, by Jay Wright

Library of Congress Cataloging-in-Publication Data

Applewhite, James.
River writing.
(Princeton series of contemporary poets)
I. Title. II. Series.
PS3551.P67R58 1988   811'.54   87-25924
ISBN 0-691-06726-0 (alk. paper)   ISBN 0-691-01442-6 (pbk.)